A Word to the Wise

30 words to renew your mind and build a lasting legacy

Andrea L Collins

ISBN: 978-0-359-38014-5 (pbk)
ASIN: B07M84MCQW

To the most prominent teachers and mentors in my life,
I am who I am because of your words.

~

To my mother, Stephanie Stamps –
your words were the first I heard and will last forever.

~

To my grandparents, Vernon & Virginia Stamps –
your love for education was contagious.

~

To my children, you are the echo of my words and remind me daily
of the importance of living intentionally.

~ CONTENTS ~

~ CONTENTS ~

"Wealth isn't about money. It's about options…
and you always have options. Choose wisely."
– Richie Norton

PREFACE

When I was a little girl I prided myself in reading the dictionary as if it were a novel. The words seemed to jump out at me and perform this eclectic, rhythmic dance that only the imagination of a young child could conjure up. It was like magic. And when I grew tired of reading, I would fold the corner of the page to ensure I was able to pick up where I left off. To further infer my level of curiosity and desire for intellectual stimulation – others may refer to this as pure nerdiness, I would read the dictionary both in English and Spanish. If I were to be completely honest with you the Spanish dictionary was an extra leap that I would often take just to create innovative ways to spark conversation with my grandfather beyond our normal daily exchanges. Because of this, one might assume that my grandfather was of Latin decent. In fact he was not. He was a black man. Born in 1928, just a few months prior to the beginning of The Great Depression. Truthfully it really did not occur to me, until I began writing this book, that this alone suggests that he must have possessed just as much of a curiosity about words as I did.

I would challenge him often. Beginning with the phrase: "I bet you don't know what this word means Granddaddy", or "I know how to spell…" His response never faltered and he would indulge my inquisitive nature every single time. In retrospect, I know those gestures had a lot to do with cultivating my own personal fascination with words and their meanings. Somehow these words served as a bridge to our relationship. It made me feel intelligent and accomplished. More importantly, it made me feel powerful.

I realize my story may not be common. I can even accept that I am probably not in large company when it comes to those who will admit to reading the dictionary as a literary piece. But there is one thing that I am sure about; effective communication is the tie that binds across the globe. Early on I learned the value in understanding how the definition of a word influences its appropriate use in speaking, writing, and day to day practicality. The application of words in our daily living not only enhances possibilities, but, encourages a deeper understanding of the function of life itself. Over my nearly 15 year career in Wealth Management I have had the opportunity to serve clients from diverse financial, cultural, ethnic, and religious backgrounds; and likewise, as many children in the same capacity of diversity as it pertains to teaching financial literacy. I have come to learn that amongst universal words - given their intended definition - the application of such to life would influence decisions that could potentially chart a different financial course for generations.

My intention for *A Word to the Wise* is twofold: to offer tools to empower you along your life course in wealth building and to enhance your vantage point of what is really important to acknowledge during the journey. All by using words. Both common and often avoided words. Words are powerful and have the ability to encourage or discourage, build up or tear down, enlighten and expose. There is no denying that who we are right now at this very moment are because of words. I remember when my children were learning to talk. Their caregiver at daycare –who happened to be a childhood friend of mine- had a phrase that she patiently encouraged them with as their communication skills began to grow. In the most loving raspy voice, she would tell them "Use your words. You have to use your words." Despite the circumstance, she would resort to this phrase. Whether it was in a state of calm exchange or within the most frustrating outbursts of a toddler trying to communicate in a language that at times seemed completely undecipherable - she insisted that it was applicable.

It is within these moments that we realize, when it comes to decision making, the vast majority of us resort to applying what we have been exposed to in life. This is widely known as selective exposure theory. Within this theory people tend to favor information that reinforces what they have already formulated opinions, beliefs and decisions around. It becomes familiar. It is comfortable. Yet, a curiosity for valuable information serves as a way to counteract selective exposure.

My curiosity with words extended far beyond my eight year old relationship with my grandfather. He died when I was in the third grade; and that was probably the only time in my life that I might have been at a loss for words. But it didn't last long, my family can attest to that. If anything my fascination grew to greater widths; I had discovered a neighbors (Fred & Welton Hickman) full set of Encyclopedia Britannica.

A few things matter most here, what you have been taught about seeking valuable information and who is coaching you through it? Lack of curiosity surrenders to the status quo and paves the way for complacency. Not to mention it is purely self-defeating.

The power of *your* words give power to those around you; more importantly to *your* family and every forthcoming generation. Accept the power. Speak intentionally and purposefully. Recognize that ancient civilizations were built and hung upon words that embodied the desire for a profound legacy. I am challenging you to do the same with your legacy. I challenge you to use *these* words as a compliment to your own.

Before you get started:

Let's take a trip down memory lane and revisit what we learned in primary education about English grammar and basic sentence parts.

Noun /noun/ a word (other than a pronoun) used to identify any of a class of people, places, or things.

Verb /vərb/ a word used to describe an action, state, or occurrence, and forming the main part of the predicate of a sentence, such as *hear, become, happen.*

Adjective /ˈajəktiv/ a part of speech which describes, identifies, or quantifies a noun or a pronoun.

Adverb /ˈadˌvərb/ a part of speech used to describe a verb, adjective, clause, or another adverb. It simply tells the readers how, where, when, or the degree at which something was done.

Throughout this book you will also be prompted with the following:

Growth application. Before you move on to understand and apply a new word, an in depth opportunity for personal growth will be explored. This is meant for a bit of introspection and to ask the questions that we sometimes gloss over when preparing for our future.

"Turn the page". This prompt is derived from the gentle nudge that I receive when I tend to get fixated on a concept or dwell in past decisions. Often times we get so caught up in the conundrum of the past that we spend more energy than necessary for what it takes to move on. It is important to gather the necessary tools and continue to build.

A word to the wise. A wise person is able to take heed to a short message and does not require a lengthy explanation to discern its meaning. There are a few short messages intertwined throughout the book.

PART I

~

INTROSPECTION

Wealth
welTH/
noun
plentiful supplies of a particular resource.
a plentiful supply of a particular desirable thing.
an abundance of valuable possessions or money.

WEALTH. When you read, hear, or speak the word *wealth,* what comes to mind?

Is it a concept that seems unattainable or within arms reach? Something in your foreseeable future or is it a long term process that you have to build up your endurance to achieve? A sprint or a marathon? An inheritance or self-actualization?

The word *wealth* carries the weight of individual significance for each and every one of us as varied and unique as our fingerprints.

What does the imprint of your personal wealth personify?
Think about it.
Keep thinking.
Keep thinking.
Nope not done yet…

Now that you have created a mental picture, what do you imagine to be the one common denominator between most wealthy individuals?

If you guessed *time*, then you are one hundred percent correct. The accumulation of wealth is built over an extended period of time. Regardless of your personification of wealth, from billionaire status to a centenarian in the amazon, the compilation of this happens through the acceptance of just how long it will take you to get there. And once you have arrived, how you will sustain it.

Think about those we read about or hear of in the news who seemingly have become an "overnight" sensation; or perhaps physically appear to be at an "optimal" level of health. The quotation of overnight and optimal was intended to highlight that the masses predominantly associate *their* sudden awareness of an individual or product as an equitable characterization of how long it actually took for the manifestation of success.

What we are not privy to is the amount of *time* – there goes that pesky word again – that has been devoted to cultivating what we see as the final result.

Committing to the distance, therefore, is simply a matter of our viewpoint of the race. Possessing an unwavering belief that building wealth is worth your time allows you to compartmentalize the effect of distance. You begin to embrace it as an inevitable part of the process. A right of passage, so to speak, riddled with a wide stretch of opportunity. Nevertheless, there is one thing for sure that you can count on -the time will pass either way.

I often used that analogy before every 1500m race that my daughter would run. If you are familiar with Track & Field you might agree that particular race is one of the most grueling. It requires an increased amount of mental stamina, not to mention hydration, proper breathing techniques, endurance, and the ability to pace yourself.

The morning of the track meets my daughter would predictably complain and I would remind her that she only had to run the race once that day. More importantly, because there was only one opportunity this was her moment to tap into all of her tools – what she had been coached on for months. The fact that she only had to run once got her every time and she would literally put her all into it. Building your wealth is something similar. It's a long distance race that is achieved best with the conscious recognition of time coupled with opportunity.

Each of us are at a different point in the race. There are some of you that might have just come out of the block, or perhaps you are on the lap where it's time to pace yourself and build up enough momentum for the final stretch, or maybe you are rounding the curve with increased speed ready to sprint towards the finish line. Wherever you are in the process do not lose sight of why you are running. **A word to the wise:** I have yet to meet one person that runs a race to lose.

"If you really look closely, overnight successes took a long time." - Steve Jobs

Growth application:

A fingerprint is an impression that is left by the friction ridges of the human finger. There are two methods in which a fingerprint can be captured; chanced impressions and deliberate impressions. A chanced impression is left on surfaces that we typically encounter daily. For instance, on glass or metal. Deliberate impressions are formed using ink and subsequently transferred onto a surface. Whether the impression is chanced or deliberate, the undeniable fact about fingerprints is that they are unique and the durability is life-long.

Similarly the impression our ideal of wealth leaves upon our family can be captured by chance or deliberately. Consider what type of imprint you are leaving behind.

Turn the page.

Perception

pər'sepSH(ə)n

noun

a way of regarding, understanding, or interpreting something; a mental impression.

PERCEPTION. Our perceptions of money, how to attain it, and how to manage it is impressed upon us at a very young age.

If we are immersed in an environment of struggle, money is perceived as scarce; while being raised in a wealth abundant environment can make room for the understanding of wealth not necessarily as a means to an end but the means to tangible and intangible freedom. Either way, the decisions we make are an absolute reflection of our beliefs.

The scarcity of money affects the decision to spend our income on urgent needs, while essentially ignoring future needs – thereby creating scarcity for tomorrow. It's a vicious cycle that those not part of a financial struggle manage to escape the entanglement of, and instead have the privilege of devoting their resources to prepare for futuristic outcomes. On a simplistic level this is why generational wealth and poverty exist.

Scarcity deals with limited resources that fuel the perpetual want or need for things. In contrast, a life of abundance defies the idea of lack and is consistently full.

Thinking back to your childhood would you define your life in scarcity or abundance? How do you define your life now?

What has shaped the difference? *Is* there a difference?

Growth application:

Our relationship with money is rooted in perception and perspective. Where do our perceptions come from? They come from our friends, social media, our colleagues, our associates to name a few. More importantly our perceptions begin with our inherent surroundings – family. Family influences our individual version of reality. And one important tool that is used to make the distinctions within our realities is language. Anthropologist Edward Sapir states "We see and hear and otherwise exercise very largely as we do because the language habits of our community predispose certain choices of interpretation." Consider the type of language centered on money and finance that you were exposed to growing up. Do any themes or sayings stand out to you?

Turn the page.

Emotions

əˈmōSH(ə)n/

noun

a natural instinctive state of mind deriving from one's circumstances, mood, or relationships with others.

EMOTIONS. When it comes to money we have to learn how to check our emotions at the door. **A word to the wise**, this is difficult for everyone.

The most common emotions that are embedded within our interaction with money are fear, shame, guilt and anger. And I'm sure most of you reading this almost immediately countered that statement with, "…but if I won the lotto or if I had a multimillion dollar business then I would not have those negative emotions about money." Not so fast. The initial elation of an abundance of money is often quickly replaced by such emotions as fear or greed. Fear and greed are two of the main emotional drivers of decision making that contributes to the loss of wealth.

Yes, your emotional behavior with money can be the source of losing what you have earned. Simply because our financial decisions are a direct reflection of our perception of money. This is the part where you may need to refer back to the previous definition on perception.

Our perceptions feed our emotions and can either contribute to a ferocious appetite of destruction or serve as nourishment for a healthy, balanced relationship.

Many people willingly admit to emotional eating habits and the temporary fix it provides. What they will also admit is the aftermath of poor health and maybe even a change in clothing size. Similarly, our emotions can show up in our bank accounts.

What are some financial decisions that you have made driven by your emotions?

They key to tackling this is **naming them** and then **taming them.**

Take a moment to identify some immediate emotions that you have centered on money.

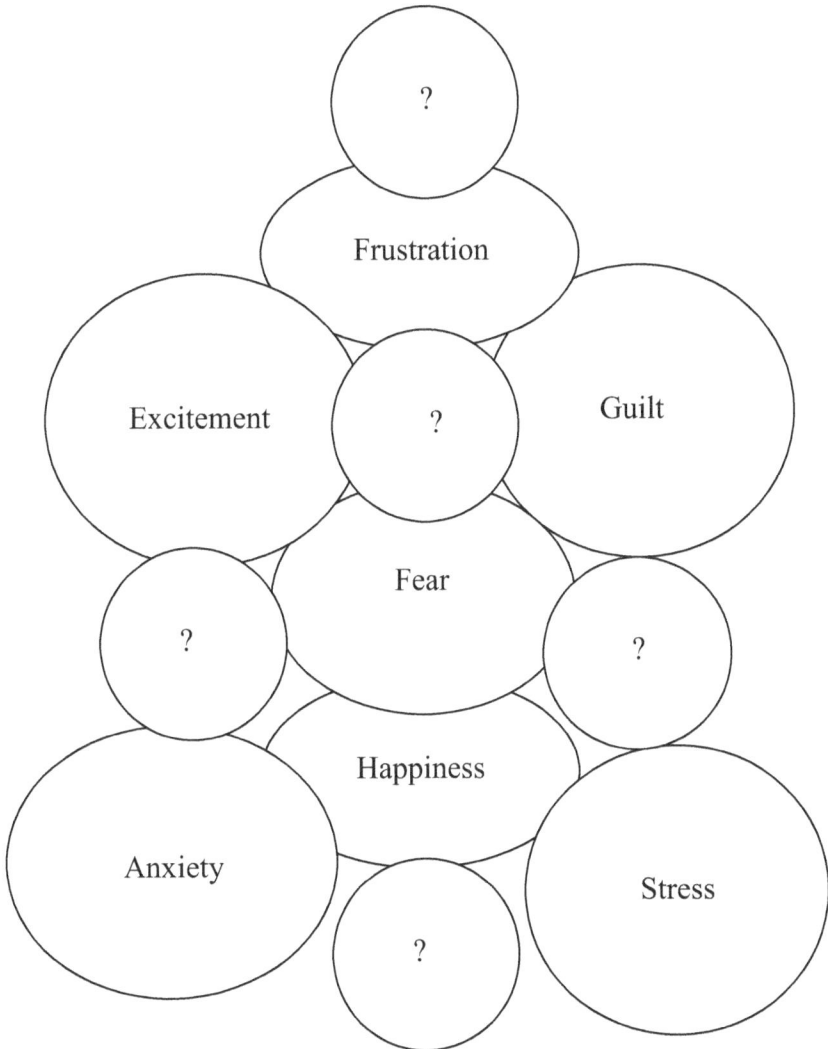

Growth application:

A lagging indicator is a measurable factor used in economics to measure changes that follow a pattern or trend. They are output driven. For example, a rise in interest rates is an indicator of a change in economic and market events – taxes, political climate, money supply, etc. Likewise, your net worth displays a measurable pattern of your financial habits. Author James Clear talks about this extensively in the book *Atomic Habits*.

To sum it up, the picture of your entire being is a measurable outcome of the patterns you have developed in your life up until this very moment. Undeniably the lagging indicators tell us, tell you, and tell me, the types of decisions we have made thus far. Furthermore, you should be able to identify the emotions behind each of your life decisions.

Consider the picture your outputs paint about your process.

OUTPUT LAGGING INDICATOR	INPUT EMOTION
(ex: Career I am unhappy with)	*Fear*
(ex: Obsessed with spending)	*Anxiety*

With this exercise it's important to work backwards, starting with your current situation in order to identify what emotions carried you to this point.

Turn the page.

Relationships

rəˈlāSH(ə)nˌSHip/

noun

the way in which two or more concepts, objects, or people are connected, or the state of being connected.

RELATIONSHIPS. If you are breathing, walking, talking, and living you have many types of relationships; family, friends, co-workers, acquaintances, our pets and even with things. Some of our relationships can tend to be superficial while others run deeper than the Pacific Ocean. Some healthy and others not so healthy. Some that make room for you to grow and others that stifle you. Some that cause so much pain and others that bring healing. We also have these types of relationships with money. I would even go as far as arguing that it is one of the most important relationships to tend to because of the role it plays in our complete wellbeing. When you think of why we gravitate towards certain people or things during specific periods in our lives it stems from what is provided by them. We may lean in on a sibling when we need to feel comfort or be our authentic selves, we may lean in spiritually to feel grounded, and we may lean into our children when we need to be reminded of what it is like to be carefree. What do you lean into money for?

Cultivating a healthy, solid connection with our resources makes a difference in how far we can go, what we are able to accomplish, and what we are able to offer others along the way.

A word to the wise: The role money plays in our complete wellbeing has nothing to do with the actual amount of dollars we have.

Before you turn the page take a moment and reflect on the words we have explored: *wealth, perception, emotions, and relationships.*

What realizations have you come to about yourself during this process? What will it take for you to move on?

Growth application:

There are four early attachment phases that psychologists use to determine how you will function in adult relationships and as a parent to your child. Secure attachment requires a child to feel securely attached to their parent or caregiver by the feeling of safety, being seen and soothed. In a secure attachment you have a relationship that is sensitive and responsive. The avoidant attachment phase involves an adult or caregiver that is emotionally unavailable and thus insensitive to the child's needs. These children tend to pull away and become self-contained. Thirdly, there is the ambivalent or anxious attachment phase. Within this phase the adult is inconsistently attuned to the child leaving them confused and insecure. Lastly, there is disorganized attachment phase. This phase deals with abuse towards a child – physical or emotional, causing distress and dissociation.

You may be wondering why the insert of these psychological terms is necessary. Our relationship with money is rooted in perception and perspective. Consider which attachment phase you experienced during your childhood and the correlation it may have with your relationship with money.

Turn the page.

PART II

~

REFRAMING

Mindset
ˈmīn(d)set/
Noun
the established set of attitudes held by someone.

MINDSET. It's no puzzle that how we are raised, along with the financial values of our parents and surroundings have a way of rubbing off on us. Whether you were privy to those dinner table conversations about banking and finance, or was forced to learn off the cuff, the way we manage our wealth is a direct descendant of what we have been exposed to.

Depending on the type of household you were raised in, adult financial behavior is a conglomerate of those beliefs, values, and methods of survival. The first step to creating a wealth driven mindset is to identify the healthy habits to maintain and how to begin to do the work of discarding those of which will inherently hinder your independence.

Your attitude determines your altitude. In other words, your financial mindset has a large impact on your ability to achieve your goals.

Scarce vs Abundant

Questions to ask yourself on identifying a scarcity mindset
- Are you afraid to spend money?
- Do you spend money as soon as you receive it?
- Do you feel as if there is never enough?

What are the indicators of an abundant mindset?
- Regardless of your financial landscape you believe that there are favorable outcomes
- You believe that you will always have enough to meet your needs

The Awareness Quadrant
Shifting towards an abundant mindset

Inside of this quadrant is where I've found you must reside in order to maintain control of the shift.

What you do not take control of will ultimately control you. **A word to the wise**, this is *not* in reference to people.

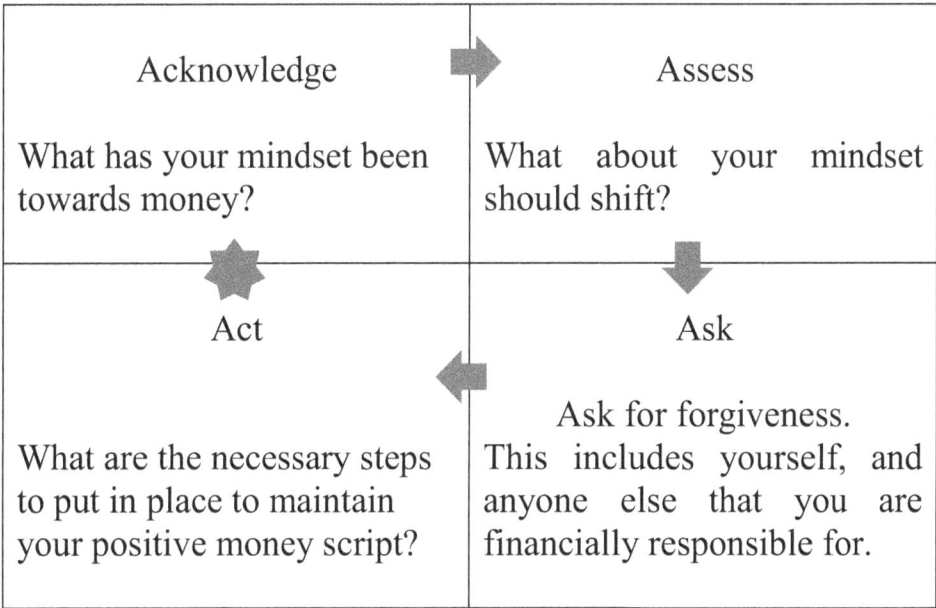

Acknowledge	Assess
What has your mindset been towards money?	What about your mindset should shift?
Act	Ask
What are the necessary steps to put in place to maintain your positive money script?	Ask for forgiveness. This includes yourself, and anyone else that you are financially responsible for.

Shifting to an abundant state of mind requires that you first acknowledge and forgive yourself for the past. Including up until this very moment.

Secondly, become the captain of the direction your money moves in. You must gain the confidence to establish a plan and be bold enough to stick to it.

Whistle a different tune by changing your money script. A negative money script is everything we've ever told ourselves or practiced that could potentially get in the way of our abundance.

"Abundance mindset is more than just a belief, it's a way of life and an attitude that is backed by action."–Jay Shetty

Growth application:

To pivot refers to the point of rotation. I think it is safe to assume that because you are reading this book that you are at a point where you believe that it is time to rotate or turn your life in another direction. When used in the example of entrepreneurship a pivot includes a shift in strategy while keeping one foot on the ground rooted in past experiences. These experiences should be used as a guidepost for roads that you no longer need to travel down and an anchor to stably forge you into a new direction.

The ability to pivot at the right time could mean the difference in immediate or delayed success. Take Instagram for example. The widely popular social media app began with another name and functionality. The company used their knowledge of user engagement centered on the photo sharing component of their app and pivoted from that information. Acknowledge a frame of mind, habit, or process that you are ready to pivot from and as Jeff Bezos suggests, "investigate everything" and "minimize the regret".

Turn the page.

Value

'valyoo/

noun

the regard that something is held to deserve; the importance, worth, or usefulness of something.

VALUE. Our values are a reflection of our authentic selves. If I were to ask you what your personal values are what would be at the top of your list?

Believe it or not, money and values fit together like a hand in glove. Often what we use money for and how adamantly we pursue our passions are predicated on the amount of money we actually believe is needed to fulfill those desires combined with how much we are willing to grind for it. Even more so, how can you effectively devise a plan for prosperity without admitting what it is you care most about?

Money is meant to be used as a tool to help us reach our goals. Fulfillment is derived from our values and our relationship with money moving in lock step.

Take a moment to contemplate what you truly value. Is your current way of life in alignment with those values?

Be honest. No judgement. Just you and your thoughts. Most importantly do not judge yourself. There's no right or wrong answer. Nothing is too lofty or unattainable.

Now, make a commitment to honoring transparency and your authentic self by creating a personal value system. This system is comprised of principles that serve as a point of reference for your behavior. It also provides a much needed structure for that internal checks and balance when determining your alignment with what is meaningful to you.

Growth application:

In 1943 Abraham Maslow proposed a psychological theory – Maslow's hierarchy of needs – in the paper "A Theory of Human Motivation". His theory has been used to study the behavioral motivation of humans and originally concluded that movement to the next level requires individual satisfaction of the current level. Over time, sociologists have identified that each level is constantly overlapping and at any given point in time a lower level may take precedence over a higher level need. Consider what your values look like in each level of Maslow's hierarchy.

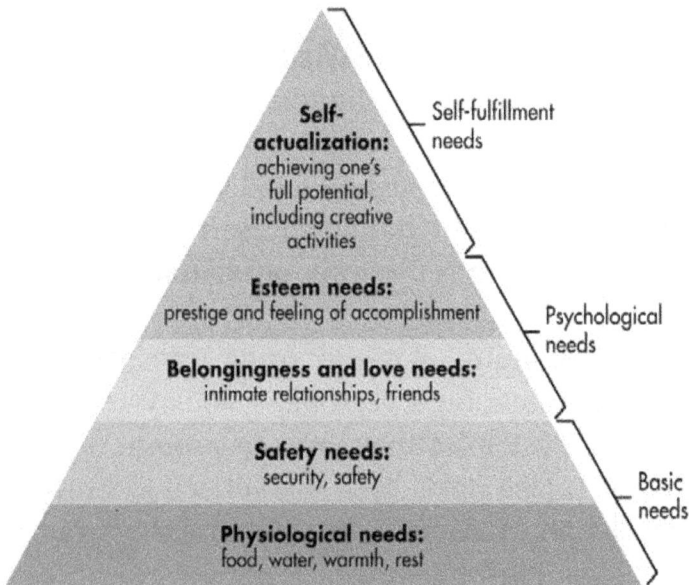

Self-fulfillment needs

Self-actualization: achieving one's full potential, including creative activities

Psychological needs

Esteem needs: prestige and feeling of accomplishment

Belongingness and love needs: intimate relationships, friends

Basic needs

Safety needs: security, safety

Physiological needs: food, water, warmth, rest

Adapted from: <u>*https://www.simplypsychology.org/maslow.html*</u>

Turn the page.

Education

ˌejəˈkāSH(ə)n/

noun

the process of receiving or giving systematic instruction, especially at a school or university.
information about or training in a particular field or subject.

EDUCATION. Now that we've turned the page on introspection, how can we begin to confidently navigate in the right direction? Having education in any subject allows us to make informed decisions. Admittedly, my primary education experience was devoid of financial literacy, and any other principles that would train students on how to build, attain, and maintain any form of wealth. We were not given guidance on how to identify what we valued or what we were exposed to when it came to developing an understanding of money. As a result, I am for certain many of our relationships with money have been through unhealthy cycles. This was a huge failure in the public education system, and thankfully there is widespread attention to this matter now. However, that does not erase the fact that we are still facing a major financial literacy problem and only five states within the United States have a personal finance requirement in high school.

This means you are responsible for seeking the education, mentorship, and advising based off of your own curiosity or finally becoming fed up with your present circumstance. Curiosity leads to discovery and discomfort leads to change.

Identify your financial pain points. The fear of the unknown can be debilitating to say the least, however, acknowledging what keeps you up at night will point you in the direction of uncovering what you do and do not know.

Ask the questions and then educate your children.
You might be surprised about what information is readily available at your fingertips starting within your immediate circle. "Money is a tool. It will take you wherever you wish, but it will not replace you as the driver." – Ayn Rand

Growth application:

Knowledge is power. This is an old adage that I am for certain you are familiar with or have heard at least once in your life time. I would agree that knowledge serves as a critical part to gaining power. But, you cannot just stop there. You have to do something with that knowledge in order for the force to be transformed into power.

Newton's second law states the force (F) acting on a body is equal to the mass (m) of the body multiplied by the acceleration (a) of its center of mass.

The basic equation of motion is $F=ma$.

As it applies to knowledge, your **Power** (*Force*) is only equal to your **Knowledge** (**m***ass*) multiplied by **Action** (**a***cceleration*).

Power = Knowledge x Action

Turn the page.

Priority
prī'ôrədē/
noun
the fact or condition of being regarded or treated as more important.
the right to take precedence or to proceed before others.

PRIORITY. Proper priorities lead you down the path to prosperity. A word to the wise: This is a great tongue twister to right down and post where you can see it daily.

It can be easy to live day to day with no real plan in place or clear idea of what is really important to you. Let alone naming those things and writing them down. Without this discipline we run the risk of not accomplishing our most important goals. Keep in mind that as our lives change, priorities shift. If you are a recent college graduate, your number one priority may be paying down student loan debt. If you are married and the parent(s) of school aged children, perhaps your priority is home ownership or paying for braces and extracurricular activities. Or you have reached the dilemma of saving for your child's college education versus your retirement. Whatever your goals are, you have to prioritize and then set the plan to tackle them. Some goals are achievable simultaneously while others may cause you to make temporary sacrifices.

List your wants versus your needs and then prioritize what you have come up with in order of importance and feasibility.

Go deep with this list. Beyond the superficial. Proper priorities always create room for opportunity in the long run.

If you are having trouble getting started here is a generic order of importance that you can build from:

Save an emergency fund
Save for retirement
Pay down debt
Invest

47

Growth application:

If you think you have suffered from the inability of being able to prioritize your personal goals, consider the fact that organizations face this challenge daily on an exponentially larger level. Studies show that the organizations that tend to flourish or outperform others are the ones that have a laser beam focus and high level of discipline when it comes to the dedication of sticking to their priorities. In an organization and in your personal life it's what matters most at any given moment in time.

Ignoring your senses of what is urgent versus what can wait will undeniably cause damage in the long run. This can be the decision between accepting a last minute call before an important meeting or spending the money to buy coffee versus saving the extra five dollars. When we don't set priorities we tend to follow the path of the least resistance. Stephen Covey suggests to divide a paper into four boxes. Label each with the following: Important and Urgent, Important and Not Urgent, Not Important but Urgent, Not Important and Not Urgent. Plug your tasks into one of the four squares and your priorities should become a lot clearer.

Turn the page.

Opportunity
ˌäpərˈt(y)o͞onədē/
noun
a set of circumstances that makes it possible to do something.

OPPORTUNITY. When is the last time opportunity knocked on your door? Were you prepared? Shocked? Skeptical? Hesitant? Cynical? I have felt all of those emotions, if not more, in each aspect of my life- educationally, professionally, and personally. Hypothetically we tend to envision ourselves moving mountains when good old opportunity comes a'knockin. My question to you is have you done the work to prepare to seize that opportunity? Would you value the opportunity if it was staring you right in the face?

If you can identify with growing up in an impoverished area opportunities may have been limited. No doubt where you are born and societal position play a pivotal role in what you have access to. It's quite possible that at some point in your life you may have been overlooked for opportunities because of your gender, race, religion, age, culture or sexuality. Often times it is merely a case of not realizing what lies in the palm of our hands until the opportunity is missed.

I'll share a quick story with you:

There once was a very wealthy and curious king. This king had a huge boulder placed in the middle of a road well-traveled. Then he hid nearby to observe if anyone would attempt to move the boulder from the road. The first group of people that passed by happened to be some of the wealthiest merchants. Rather than moving it, they simply walked around it. Some of those that passed by cursed the king for neglecting the roads and blamed him for the huge rock as an obstacle. Yet, none of these people tried to move the boulder. Finally, a lone man came along. His arms were full of vegetables. When he approached the boulder he set the vegetables down and with all his might pushed it to the side. As he picked back up his load he noticed a bag lying in the road where the boulder had been. It was full of gold coins and a note. The king had written the note and stated that is was a reward for moving the boulder out of the middle of the road.

What we are able to glean from this is that every obstacle opens the door for an opportunity that can drastically improve our lives. There may not literally be a pot of gold at the end of the rainbow, but what about that career you desire, or business you have dreamt about, or educational goal you have. I urge you to go after it fervently. There will definitely be obstacles in the middle of the road. What matters most is your willingness to identify your strength in moving them to the side. **A word to the wise:** you are not the only person who benefits from this. Everyone else along the path can now walk down free and clear of that specific obstacle with easier access to opportunity.

Growth application:

Carpe diem! Or shall I say, seize the opportunity. Opportunity is the synergy of time and place. It is the ultimate chance that you are granted towards receiving the momentum that's needed for the next phase of your life and comes in all forms and size. Expansion, growth, and improvement require the ability to take a risk in engaging with the unknown. In order to actively pursue opportunity you must commit to being present. In the day in age where obsession with technology pervades our lives – our devices and social media, remaining fully present may present itself to be a challenge. Identifying opportunity simply requires an intentional shift in focus. At this moment you may be thinking of lost opportunities. Do your present self a favor and…

Turn the page.

Cultivation

ˌkəltəˈvāSH(ə)n/

noun

break up (soil) in preparation for sowing or planting. prepare and use (land) for crops or gardening.

CULTIVATION. The word cultivation is often used to describe the way a farmer takes care of his crops. In farming there is a process to cultivation: decide what to grow, till the land, sow the seed, water the crop, weed and kill the pests. Likened to a farmer, we are responsible for the preparation, attention, care and pruning of our lives. Most importantly our financial sustainability.

Let's unpack the process of cultivation together.

Deciding what to grow. Aside from having a preference on what type of crop you want to grow and fruit you want to yield, you must confirm that the land you possess is conducive to what you are growing. You cannot successfully grow an apple orchard in an environment that is appropriate for rice. What type of financial landscape are *you* working with? This will indicate what you are ready to begin cultivating. You may feel limited at this point but stand firm in knowing that you are just getting started.

The next step is **tilling the land.** Farmers typically till the land by loosening the soil with the appropriate tools and mixing in fertilizers that add important nutrients for the soil. Why do they take the time to add things to the soil? One would think that the soil was equipped to do what it does, right? Not necessarily. Based on the environment, hazards, and a host of other circumstances breaking up the hardened land and providing additional resources preps the land for optimal results. Likewise, what old habits have you settled into that needs to be tilled in order to allow you to receive seeds that need to be planted? What extra nourishment is required in order to create a healthy environment susceptible to growth?

Sowing the seed. Early farmers sewed seed by broadcasting or throwing seed by hand over the entire field. Naturally, with the evolution of modern technology, there are machines that now do the heavy lifting. Nevertheless, the process in which we receive information is null and void if the first two steps are omitted. Often times we treat valuable knowledge like throwing spaghetti on the wall and waiting to see what sticks. Cultivating a financially sustainable life requires an intentional, methodical process.

Watering the crop. At this point of cultivation the preparation has been completed. And the final step prior to waiting is watering. The imperative thing to gage in this stage is how much water is necessary. How do you know? By learning what is appropriate for the fruit you are trying to yield, combined with the season, the climate, the weather from the year prior to name a few. This is very specific and measured. Too much can yield an over saturated crop, and too little can yield to a dry environment that is not productive for growth.

Weeding and killing pests. You have managed to cultivate your crop. It is plentiful and abundant. But your work is far from done. While you may indulge in reaping the benefits of what you have sown, you must now work to maintain the viability of your crop. Weeding and killing pests is a proactive and defensive tactic. Again, this is optimized by studying and becoming an expert on your crop. At this point in order to maintain the viability you cannot afford to be unaware of what could potentially attack it. Likewise, when it comes to our financial health, we must maintain one step ahead of what could potentially destroy what we have worked so diligently to harvest.

Growth application:

One term that often gets correlated with cultivation is *relationships*. Investing time into building our personal lives should be coupled with building beneficial relationships with others that add mutual value. Take a moment to evaluate the effort you have placed on nurturing beneficial relationships in your life.

Meaningful relationships play a vital role in overall well-being. Researchers have found that there are two types of support that are gained from close relationships: the ability to thrive through adversity and thriving in the absence of adversity – meaning support in embracing and pursuing opportunities. What has your cultivation process reaped?

Turn the page.

Strategy

ˈstradəjē/

noun

a plan of action or policy designed to achieve a major or overall aim.

the art of planning and directing overall military operations and movements in a war or battle.

STRATEGY.

Let's take a deep dive into the definition of *strategy*. These words pack a punch on their own:

- Plan
- Action
- Designed
- Achieve
- Aim
- Art
- Directing
- Movement
- War

While *strategy* is a noun, the words used to complete the definition are verbs. This means that behind your strategy is action and should always be formed in advance. Devising a good strategy will dictate how you travel along the journey of building wealth. Realizing that no two journeys are alike, the pace at which you design and implement your strategy is solely dependent on identifying the criteria necessary at this moment in time. Strategic plans are dynamic and should be able to adapt to unexpected life events leaving room for updates and shifts.

Before you begin devising your strategy take a moment to answer a few questions:

Are the criteria for success in place?

Think ahead about the overall direction you are pointing yourself or your family in, take inventory of your resources, objectively acknowledge your strengths and weaknesses - along with potential external obstacles, and confirm that your strategy reaches who it should benefit with the end result.

What do I want to avoid?
The most important thing to avoid is devising a strategy that does not ultimately contribute to your mission, vision or objective.

Use the **3T End Result** table to jumpstart your strategy.

End Result: *(i.e. savings of $10,000)*

Team	Tools	Timeframe
Banker *Accountability* *partner*	*Savings account* *Budget*	*1 year*

Growth application:

I once read that the best way to develop a winning strategy is to study history. Throughout my educational journey the subject of history by far has been one of my favorites. Particularly because it is so interesting to plot the similarities and differences between the winners, the losers, and the overcomers. I would even join the masses in the belief that history repeats itself and if you are unaware of the past you are most certainly doomed to repeat it. When you are attempting to devise a winning wealth plan you must study the strategies of those that have achieved similar successes as well as the pitfalls of others.

Think about the development of babies. They learn to crawl, walk, talk and eat by modeling the behavior of those around them. This practice is known as *conscious observance*. As life goes on, the eagerness and tenacity that we possessed as a young child manages to escape us. I encourage you to humbly return to your inner child and make a list of those you will consciously observe at this very moment.

Turn the page.

PART III

~

RECONSTRUCTING

Balance

ˈbaləns/

noun

an even distribution of weight enabling someone or something to remain upright and steady.

BALANCE. Have you ever taken a yoga class and been able to hold warrior pose, tree pose, or any pose for that matter that requires you to take at least one foot off of the ground? Or watched in awe at gymnasts who confidently trot across the beams and stick their landings on the mats? How about a baseball pitcher's stance as he pivots to throw the ball? There is one thing that is the culprit behind all of this. *Balance*. And as the definition states, to balance is to maintain an even distribution of weight.

Aside from athletes balancing in sport, everyday people spend their lives balancing time, activities, commitments, work/life, their finances and a host of other things that require even measure in order to achieve optimal results. This even measure does not just employ itself haphazardly or fall out of the sky. It takes intentional effort, dedication, and practice. I remember the first time – actually the first few times – which I attempted to balance in a yoga pose. It was riddled with wobbling and shaking, not to mention often drifting and falling over to my side.

The yoga instructor, who happened to be my sister, constantly encouraged me to find my center. Once I got past taking instruction from my younger sister (cannot help the birth order characteristics), I began to do what most people do that are successful in balancing their weight. Focus. I focused with a burning desire to achieve that optimal state.

As long as you have experienced the state of being balanced at least one time in your life, it is utterly impossible to forget what that feels like. You possess the ability to return to that position by applying the same intention.

When we consider our financial stability, balance is important because it is indicative of a level of self-control and attention. It allows us to move through our lives confidently knowing that our stability rests on two things: a solid foundation and proportionate weight.

Growth application:

Something to consider when balancing is the foundation on which you are attempting to balance on. The smaller the surface underneath the less stable it will be, requiring you to use more balance. What is your financial foundation? More so, what additional weight have you placed on that foundation? Is it sturdy enough to bear your decision making?

Turn the page.

Discipline
ˈdisəplən/
noun
a system of rules of conduct.

DISCIPLINE. Wealth is a cumulative result of many habits, disciplines, and practices added together and compounded over a lifetime. Think about what happens to our children (or anyone's for that matter) when they lack discipline. The failure of this often results in children that are resentful, unhappy, and lacking the tools necessary to navigate through life challenges and relationships. The same goes for us while in the process of building wealth; without financial discipline we can grow into resentful, unhappy adults – eventually unable to navigate through life's challenges.

But just as important as whether or not we are disciplined, is *how* we discipline ourselves.

And not typical authoritarian discipline. Specifically because an authoritative style bleeds characteristics of high demand and low responsiveness. Our goal is to win and steer clear of creating patterns of unreasonable expectations.

I remember feeling the frustration of wanting to be at a certain place in my life financially based on societal norms or standards. There is this undeniable amount of pressure placed amongst all of us that says you must graduate by *this* age, in order to attain *this* by *that* age, and then be able to accomplish *this* by *this* age. And if you don't... Then you're entire existence has been wasted. My personal frustration was capitalized by the environment I worked in. From my early twenties on I was exposed to this massive amount of wealth that our clients had attained by many different means; through entrepreneurship, legacy, or just plain old hard work. I managed these accounts daily in complete awe; constantly wondering what it took for them to get to this point. The one common denominator was discipline. Discipline in decision making. Discipline in monitoring their spending. Discipline in acquiring knowledge. Discipline in communication. Discipline in maintaining what they had earned thus far. Discipline in sticking to their purpose. Discipline. Discipline. Discipline.

And then there came a time that I had to be completely honest with myself and admit that I lacked the discipline. Why? People are not born with self-discipline. It is something that is taught; a learned behavior. Discipline is what provides strength to push past the hardships in life and the decision to do what we *should* do versus what we want to do. Similar to any other skill you may have tried to master, discipline requires practice. Practicing executing your willpower which is only as strong as you perceive it to be and only as valuable as the worth you have placed on your long term goal(s).

Growth application:

One thing that tends to serve as a great compliment to maintaining discipline is the anticipation of achieving your goal. Reminding yourself of what is at the end of the tunnel will eventually cause you to build up enough momentum to actually get there. You have to start somewhere. Why not here? Now move forward with small, doable steps until you reach the finish line.

"Discipline is the difference between what you want now and what you want most." - Unknown

Turn the page.

Patience

pāSHəns/

noun

the capacity to accept or tolerate delay, trouble, or suffering without getting angry or upset.

PATIENCE. Patience is a virtue. As Warren Buffet said "Successful investing takes time, discipline and patience. No matter how great the talent or effort, some things just take time: You can't produce a baby in one month by getting nine women pregnant." (No pun intended)

A few years of my early childhood was spent living in Las Cruces, New Mexico. I would admit that all of my grade school teachers left a lasting impression on me in a variety of ways, but there is one particular teacher that I think of often. Not a month goes by that I am not reminded of her in some fashion or form. Her name was Mrs. Green. It was the early 80's, I was always eager to learn and soaked up every ounce of instruction and wisdom. Did I fail to mention it was a Pre-K class? Yep, lots of wisdom going on in there. I bring mention to that jokingly, however, in all honesty that is where most children receive the reinforcement of life skills and lessons.

I can vividly picture my teacher's plump face with those round glasses and fluffy hair – I did say it was the 80's. For some reason her age was non-descript then and still is in my opinion; but if I had to guess it would probably be in her mid to late 40's. Heaven forgive me if I am wrong. Mrs. Green had this life altering practice that I happily inducted into my daily routine and still visualize today. She developed a profound method of instilling patience in us four year olds. Her technique was simple yet effective. In the beginning of the school year she gifted all of us miniature care bears in varied colors. We were to keep the bears inside of our desks and at the very moment we sensed ourselves becoming frustrated with a situation or classwork we were to pull the bears out of the desk cubby and place it on top of our desks in clear view. Named our "patience bear", not a day went by that the bears did not make an appearance.

It became a game of recognition at the age of four. And an opportunity to correct any ounce of impatience that would knock us off course. Mrs. Green was my last teacher in Las Cruces before moving back to Los Angeles, but what she instilled in me is a virtue I have carried with me for a lifetime. Have I lost patience at times? Absolutely. Will I grow impatient ever again? Absolutely. But that is far from the point. Patience as a virtue represents a behavior. Behaviors take practice and require an intentional focus. For my four year old self the bear was the focal point.

Financially speaking what is your focal point that causes you to course correct? Could it be saving enough for your dream home, or your kid's college tuition, or even a vacation that you have desired for quite some time? None of this will come without the ability to tolerate or accept the path that it will take you to get there.

Growth application:

Have you ever heard the phrase "Rome wasn't built in a day"? What does that mean to you? Often times I believe we walk around spewing out popular phrases and memes without truly internalizing where these messages are derived from. As majestic and beautiful as the city of Rome is, the sustainability of grandeur was predicated on measured patience in the laying of bricks literally every hour. Important work undeniably takes time. What in your financial future is worth the time?

Turn the page.

Delayed gratification
dəˈlā/
verb
postpone or defer (an action).

grat·i·fi·ca·tion
ˌgradəfəˈkāSH(ə)n/
noun
pleasure, especially when gained from the satisfaction of a desire

DELAYED GRATIFICATION. Delayed gratification requires that we put off an immediate or temporary happiness by instituting practices in the present that are sacrificial. To some the thought of sacrifice may sound like such an unappealing word. If you ever want to see the devil rear its ugly head try spending a day teaching children about delayed gratification. And not just any children. YOUR children. If you have mastered this then you have solved one of parentings greatest mysteries. How to successfully navigate through any store without your child asking for something on every aisle.

Am I in this camp alone, or can you identify with having a conversation with your child prior to going into an establishment? If you have, it may start off something similar to this: "I am only going in here to get…" or "Do not ask me for anything in here, we only came to buy…" For some odd reason they always agree. At least my children do. Until they plant both feet two steps past the entrance. It's as if they become possessed and everything we just discussed gets lost in the combustion of "things". Things on every aisle, in every cart, and on every wall. Somehow, they begin to strongly desire these "things". And it's not limited to toys. I still can't figure out why my then eight year old son needed a caulking glue gun holster from Home Depot. They spend minutes attempting to convince you that they *need* these things. And not only do they need it, but they might die without it. If you don't comply then you have just become the meanest, most unfair parent to grace the earth. Slow hand clap if that is you as a parent. What about you as a kid? Are you still that kid today?

In order to practice delayed gratification you have to understand the importance of it and then fight with every fiber of your being the urge to defy that understanding. Let's be honest. The process of delayed gratification is not fun. It's purely your vision of the future that keeps you in the race. It can be likened to watching someone eat a one scoop Thrifty's ice cream cone on a hot sweltering day, knowing that you have enough to buy that same one scoop cone, but if you wait a little while longer you can buy an entire gallon of ice cream to last the many days of summer to come. That is a laymen's term example for delayed gratification but easily translatable into any aspect of your life. What will you postpone today for something greater in the future?

Growth application:

In the previous example I mentioned Thrifty's ice cream. My grandfather would take me there weekly. Depending on the era you grew up in, you may or may not be familiar with the nostalgic taste of Thrifty's. If not then just insert your favorite ice cream shop. What's your favorite flavor? For me I could not resist the temptation of mint chocolate chip or butter pecan. Part of the process of delayed gratification is understanding your temptations and why they exist. Could it be habit? What about environment or influence? Spend some time sorting through the temptations that make it tough for you to not waver when it comes to your wealth plan. Realistically, wealth is a form of delayed gratification.

Turn the page.

Planning
'planiNG/
noun
the process of making plans for something.

PLANNING. Many advise to treat your financial goals like a business and have a formal plan. There are proven business principles that lead to success: discipline and accountability, accuracy in spending patterns, leveraging and competitive advantage – all conditions that make you better than your opponent. And for the record, your opponent in this instance, is not your friend, not your colleague, not your neighbor, not your spouse – it's your present self-versus your future self.

There are three major types of planning: operational, strategic and tactical.

Strategic plans are designed to achieve your long term goals. These plans generally serve as the framework for your day to day decision making. Tactical plans are designed for immediate impact and tend to serve as a defense against any obstacle that threatens you from fulfilling your long term vision. Operational planning is the bridge between the two; it initiates the "how".

I am for certain that you are familiar with the saying "if you fail to plan, you plan to fail". Think back to the most meaningful moments in your life. Perhaps it's a marriage, a birth, a graduation, or even an interview that led to your dream job. We don't embark upon those moments without planning what we are going to do, what we will say, how we will behave, or even what we will wear. The same amount of detail must be emphasized when we consider our financial future. Without a plan in place to help your wealth grow it's easy for it to become finite. It is important to take inventory of your skills and when necessary to engage others in the process.

Growth application:

Before a building is constructed an architect or an engineer creates a detailed drawing called a blueprint. This design is an integral part to the construction of all structures. Without the plan, and the collaboration between the architect and engineer, the structure has the potential to lack safety and continuity. This will ultimately prohibit the building of a sustainable outcome. When the blueprint is created the engineer determines what materials are needed to achieve the goal of the architect. Similarly, we have to incorporate others into our planning. Who have you consulted with to ensure you have the proper tools and materials to execute your plan? Would you consider yourself to be the architect or the engineer?

Turn the page.

Saving

'sāviNG/

adjective

preventing waste of a particular resource.

SAVING. Depending on the generation you were born in the idea of saving probably causes different sentiments to arise. Consider those that survived the Great Depression. Saving didn't include the concept of socking away extra income; it was all about creating longevity of what one already had. The probability of anything extra was unlikely. In this day and age we might classify it as being frugal, yet saving for that generation was birthed out of an appreciation of affording the bare necessities of life. The baby boomer generation, however, seemingly suffers from the inability to adequately save because of an inhibition that was deplorable to those coming out of the Great Depression – debt. The difference between the two is that the latter was not faced with a scarce economy. Educational opportunities were vast, housing opportunities were affordable, and job offers were bountiful. Thus paving the way for debt accumulation.

For the Baby Boomer generation and beyond, the concept of saving at times may seem utterly impossible. Not to mention, there are endless theories on saving that range from paying yourself first, to paying yourself a set percentage, to goals based saving. You may be wondering which one is right? All of them. More importantly, you have to choose which one is right for you? The beauty in navigating your financial journey is that you get to decide. The power is in your hands. I can identify times in my life when I felt completely incapable of saving anything. It seemed that the entire amount of my monthly earnings were accounted for before it hit my account. Painstakingly I wasn't included as a benefactor in what was accounted for. A conversation I had one day with a teller at the bank further drives this point home. In the midst of the transaction he routinely asked if I had plans for the weekend.

Because it was right after Thanksgiving, my answer summed up to holiday shopping. Naturally, I returned the inquiry and his response might be shocking to most but to me sounded all too familiar. He had no plans, because as he stated he was broke and his money earned had already been ushered out of his account by auto pay. That good old auto pay feature. Yes, it keeps the lights on, but is a constant reminder of your current financial situation. My point here is that regardless of how much you earn no one ever gets to keep one hundred percent of it. Not even the wealthiest of the wealthiest.

Until then you have to come to some conclusion about where you rank in relation to your debtors, creditors and any other financial obligation that you may be consumed with. Do you believe that you owe it to your future self to save?

Growth application:

Can you identify someone close to you that you would consider to be a master saver? I can. Whenever I think of this person the level of discipline they have in saving almost seems supernatural. I used to observe in awe because the practice came like second nature. I admired it then and in retrospect still do. Growing up I was not advertently taught how to save and I believe that this is not an easy habit to acquire on your own. I'm not saying that it's impossible, it's just not easy. It takes sheer will and determination and often times it may feel as if you are going against the very fabric of your being. So, where does the discipline to save come from? It comes from a momentous realization that there is something greatly desirable in the future and followed by a decision to chart a path in that direction. For some, the future may present itself in as little as six months and equate to a tangible item. For others, the future means thirty years from now and involves a certain lifestyle during retirement. All in all, what is the one thing you desire for your future that you know requires undeniable discipline to attain? Now go for it and keep your eyes on the prize.

Turn the page.

Diversification

də͵vərsəfəˈkāSH(ə)n, *noun*
the action of making or becoming more diverse or varied.

dīˈvərs/*adjective*
showing a great deal of variety; very different.

DIVERSIFICATION. Diversity comes in many forms: gender, culture, race, religion, sexual orientation, exposure, and experience to name a few. There are so many benefits to diversity within our immediate environments that countless amounts of books have been written on the topic, corporations have launched initiatives surrounding the subject, and organizations have forged alliances to promote it. Diversity is the undisputable method behind achieving optimal success and overall sustainability.

It is beyond difficult to maintain your wealth the same way you went about earning it. Financially speaking this requires one of the most basic principles of investment: diversification. While you may understand the concept of not putting all your eggs in one basket, maybe you are not so sure of how to go about doing it. Preserving wealth requires a diversifying strategy with a long term outlook. There are many ways to diversify your wealth such as, equity investments, real estate and business ownership. To some, this may look like going outside the usual suspects and perhaps delving into the world of art or beyond the local shores. Nevertheless, diversified assets should include investments whose change in value are connected to different factors of causation. Different levels of influence are what drive performance. At its core, it is a simple technique for risk management. This often times must involve reorganization and designing specific methods of sustaining what you have accumulated with minimal unnecessary risks. To put it plainly, diversification reduces the overall probability of what you have worked so hard to attain tanking in one fell swoop.

Growth application:

"Diversity is the art of thinking independently together." – Malcolm Forbes

The best thing about diversity is amazingly articulated by Malcolm Forbes. For one it is an art. Secondly you get to remain independent. Thirdly it's collaborative. In essence diversification is one big melting pot of authentic selves. I don't know about you but that sounds like magic to my ears. If that is the case why is the acceptance or tolerance of diversity so hard to come by? I would argue that one of the main reasons is that most of us do not realize that diversification does not require you to deny who *you* are. And many of us are just downright afraid. We have fear of the strength of others. We have fear that we may shrink in the shadows. We have fear that we may not be able to rise to the occasion. And the list goes on and on. This same fear is what causes us to remain in circles of people, circumstances, and environments that resemble what is familiar. Unfortunately residing in close quarters of similarity stifles our growth. Take a look at your surroundings. Is there diversity? Why or why not? What about your financial picture. Have you pigeon holed yourself into limited exposure? What can you change?

Turn the page.

PART IV

~

REBRANDING

Purpose

ˈpərpəs/

noun

the reason for which something is done or created or for which something exists.
a person's sense of resolve or determination.

PURPOSE. "The person without a purpose is like a ship without a rudder." -Thomas Carlyle

Whether you have ever sailed a boat, or even been on a boat to say the least, it's pretty common knowledge that one of the most important parts is its rudder. The rudder is an underwater blade that is used for steering into a particular direction. Based off of its positioning, when turned, it causes the vessel's head to turn in the same direction. When a rudder is broken or damaged you may haphazardly end up in an unintended location.

Just like a ship *you* have an internal rudder. Something that guides your reason for being. Your reason for living. Even your reason for reading this book. When that guide is convoluted or not well understood then we tend to move through life aimlessly. And often look up suddenly to ask the question of how did I end up here? You might not be surprised to know that one of life's major quests is finding your purpose. I often wondered if everyone has the same curiosity then who has the answer. Well. It's simple. We all have the key to unlock our own secret box. While on the surface there may be two or more purposes that look just alike, the fact of the matter is that there is so much uniqueness nestled into that internal rudder of yours that it is utterly impossible for your purpose to be identical to any other being.

When considering your life's purpose who or what comes to mind? Or what about starting with a simpler question. When you wake up every morning what do you hope to accomplish throughout the day? And what do you eventually want all of these days to amount to? For me getting up every day and fulfilling my motherly duties is a portion that I hope amounts to something greater than what my mind can imagine. Likewise my career also fulfills another huge part of my purpose. Every day I am immersed in an environment that inhabits constant exposure to financial markets and economic factors. I am able to glean information that is then valuable to my clients, my community, my family and myself. Yes, the majority of the knowledge is available in publications available to the general public. But, in order for my individual purpose to be fulfilled, I would argue that this environment was necessary.

A concrete understanding of your purpose guides your day to day decision making. Don't get me wrong – this does not mean you are exempt from frustration or uncertainty that arises during shifting circumstances. But keep in mind that external factors are beyond your control. Much like the weather when sailing across seas; there are times when the weather is optimal and then there are storms. As long as your rudder is strong you can navigate through any situation knowing that the course you have set out on will ultimately land you exactly where you want to be.

Growth application:

What is your purpose for building wealth? Have you truly thought about it? If you have a family the first thing that may come to mind is a comfortable life for your spouse and children. Contrary to popular belief that's not everyone's desire. Some have discovered their purpose for amassing wealth is to give it away to the less fortunate. While some want to be able to do both. The great thing about it is there is no right or wrong answer. Your purpose is the bridge between inaction and action. Movement is birthed from desire. One thing that you can trust is that your purpose comes jam packed with a boat load of desire, will and determination. So what is it? What is your purpose? Don't stop asking yourself until *you've* answered the question.

A Word to the Wise: The average life expectancy in North America for males born in 2018 is 28,105 days and 29,565 days for females – 77 and 81 years respectively. Knowing your purpose adds a sense of peace. I don't know about you, but, I'd choose thousands of days of peace over anything else.

Turn the page.

Intention
in'ten(t)SH(ə)n/
noun
a thing intended; an aim or plan.

INTENTION. Acknowledging your intentions as it pertains to your own financial freedom and how it ultimately creates a path of wealth transfer for future generations is imperative.

Initially when I hear terms such as mindfulness or intention I drift towards an idea of individual practice. I envision myself in a space with the clear opportunity to achieve, receive, and distribute to others what has been given to me, with the understanding that although I would like to think of myself as awesome enough to become immortal, that in reality our days on this earth are in fact numbered.

And I'll be honest, after working in the financial services industry for nearly fifteen years, it is still apparent that the majority of us do not like to plan for our lives coming to an end. Believe it or not more than thirty percent of people do not have a wealth transfer plan. But, the intentionality behind transferring wealth is less about death and more about securing your family wealth for more than one generation; it's an act of selflessness. Done properly your grandchildren's children will eat fruit from the trees planted with your seeds.

Redirecting your focus back to your long term wealth transfer plans will serve both you and your family well and should include the following:

Intentional communication and dialogue – secures the transfer of values.

Depending on the type of family you grew up in intentional communication about future plans may or may not have been a part of your common interaction. If you did receive that then you more than likely understand the importance of informing those closest to you about what your intentions are for the financial decisions that you have made and are making. I have made it a personal practice to inform my children about the aim of my choices. For instance, I have open conversations about sacrifices that are made for futuristic outcomes. Constant dialogue opens the floodgates for questions, especially if you have smaller children. But, that's the point of communication; to arrive at a point of mutual understanding for the purpose of informed decision making.

Intentional education – secures the sustainability of wealth.

We talked about the importance of education in defining the seventh word. Instruction must be systematic and of course intentional if your goal is long term wealth transfer. Often times generational wealth transfers are not successful because of the lack of understanding of what it takes to maintain what has been inherited. Be intentional with your preservation techniques by carving out the time to teach what you know and learn together what you don't.

Intentional planning – secures the foundation that your wealth was built upon.

I just have one question. Do you have a plan for how everything you own will be distributed to your heirs? If your answer is yes, you may move on to the next intention. I have been privy to some of the most heartbreaking familial battles that could have been prevented with one simple directive. Often times even the best of intentions cannot be executed if there is no formal arrangement. Trust me, you cannot afford to put this off another day. Huge portions of estates tend to be eroded when you have no choice but to involve the court system as an intermediary.

Intentional revisiting of your plans – secures current desires are upheld.

Let's just be honest. We live in a day and age where the divorce rate unfortunately is at an all-time high. Blended families are becoming a norm, children become estranged, and over time relationships change. The one thing that is often forgotten about is to have these changes reflected on your financial documents. When is the last time you reviewed your designated beneficiaries? I make this a practice every year. Not just because of potential changes in relationship dynamics, but also because of technology glitches. Yes, technology fails us at times and it never hurts to double check for accuracy.

Intentional relationships with advisors – secures the continuity of reaching goals.

I like to think of those that serve me in an advisory capacity as accountability partners. Whatever your financial intentions are be transparent with those you have chosen to surround you. This is the only way that they are able to aid you in reaching your full potential. Remember you're in this thing together.

Growth application:

One of the most common times to set life intentions is at the beginning of the year. For the most part many of us look at January 1 as an automatic reset date. Well if you happen to be reading this on any other date besides the first of January then what are you going to do? Wait until that date rolls around again? Absolutely not. We are setting our intentions today my friend. How? By being intentional with our intentions. The Chopra center reminds us that intentions are the seed form of that which you aim to create. They can't grow if you hold onto them. With the below image in mind, what are some seeds of intention resting in the palm of your hand that you envision blossoming?

Turn the page.

Vision

'viZHən/

noun

the ability to think about or plan the future with imagination or wisdom.
the faculty or state of being able to see.

VISION. When I was a child I had a vision for my life. When I went away to college at the University of California, Berkeley I had a vision for my life then too. After my first relationship I had a vision for my life. When I started my career I had a different vision for my life. When I became a parent I crafted yet another vision for my life. After I turned thirty, you guessed it, I had a vision for my life. When I experienced the loss of family and friends my vision shifted then too. The point I am trying to make is that our lives, circumstances, and the reality of what we are up against is ever changing. During each period of change within our lives the vision we have more than likely changes right along with it. Just by the sheer definition alone our scope of perspective is widened with imagination and wisdom based on experience.

What you envision for your life either shrinks or expands with the freedom you allow yourself to see past your current circumstances. In particular, negative financial situations have a tendency to suck the air out of what you imagine your possibilities to accrue. If you are living paycheck to paycheck it can be hard to envision a life of immeasurable comfortability. I am here to tell you that it is possible and has everything to do with the permission you grant yourself to believe. If belief is not your struggle, then it may be time to recalibrate your vision for yourself and future generations. Often times when we achieve our goals we dwell in that success without acknowledging the need for going back to the drawing board. You're not finished yet. As long as there is breath in your body there's more to be accomplished in securing your future and your legacy.

At this very moment in your life what is your vision for your financial future?

I'll share mine: *That my financial decisions today will serve as the catalyst for change in my family towards building sustainable wealth beyond my immediate offspring.*

I would argue that the vision for your life should be taken as seriously as the vision for well-known successful companies and organizations. Here are a few to consider:

Amazon: "Our vision is to be earth's most customer centric company; to build a place where people can come to find and discover anything they might want to buy online."

Disney: "To be one of the world's leading producers and providers of entertainment and information."

Nordstrom: "To give customers the most compelling shopping experience possible."

Tesla: "To accelerate the world's transition to sustainable energy."

Habitat for Humanity: "A world where everyone has a decent place to live."

Teach for America: "One day, all children in this nation will have the opportunity to attain an excellent education."

The best vision statements tend be clear, concise and inspirational.

Rules of thumb:

- Your vision statement is a declaration
- Your vision statement guides your decision making
- Your vision statement is a reflection of your highest hopes in the long term
- Your vision statement is future based- the end goal is bigger than today
- Your vision statement should inspire
- Your vision statement is a living document

Growth application:

Why does a vision statement matter? It has been proven that crafting a vision statement creates a surge in engagement for all of those involved. When you are creating your vision statement don't lock it up and throw away the key. Share your vision with your family and make it all inclusive. The benefits of making it public creates concrete opportunities for buy in and support. Not to mention an immense sense of pride when that vision is realized.

Turn the page.

Mission
ˈmiSHən/
noun
a strongly felt aim, ambition, or calling.

MISSION.
Mission accomplished. Mission impossible. Mission aborted.

These are some common phrases or tag lines that come to mind when I think of the word mission. I'm not sure why but my imagination always drifts into this epic movie scene where I am on this exhilarating quest to fulfill a calling. And I've experienced all three outcomes above, both literally and figuratively. Let's take a moment to unpack them a bit more in detail.

Mission accomplished
This is that gratifying moment when the goal you set to achieve gets checked off the list. Accomplished with diligence and defeat of any and all obstacles.

Mission impossible
There are some goals that you have set to accomplish that you realize are impossible at this moment – be careful not to insinuate indefinitely – due to limited resources. This is when you need to readjust the mission by incorporating others into the process so that the goal can eventually be achieved.

Mission aborted
I can clearly hear the commander over the loud speaker screaming, Abort Abort! That commander is you. That commander is me. Have you ever ended something prematurely? I have. This is typically initiated when there is forseeable danger or detriment to your overall wellbeing. Sometimes ideas that looked great on paper or initially sounded good turn out to be not what we intended midstream. Do not be

so committed to your original understanding that you fail to stop and reset.

A word to the wise about creating your personal mission statement:

This should clearly communicate what it is that you do. For all intents and purposes it serves as your "why". Mission statements are meant to keep you aligned with your values and vision for your future. Start by asking yourself what is important to you and the type of legacy you want to leave.

My personal mission statement: *To create personal finance educational tools that transcend culture, race, gender and age.*

Growth application:

Everything you do typically should fit within the boundaries of your mission statement. If it sounds restrictive, it's because it is. But not in a way where you feel trapped. After all you are the one creating the boundaries. Let's do this in a three-step process:

1. Declare your mission
2. Start living it daily by reading it aloud
3. Hold yourself accountable by revisiting it often

A Word to the Wise: Mission and Vision statements are not only for adults. This year my oldest son began high school and I encouraged him to create both. Since we are always on the go, we keep his handwritten statement (nothing fancy) on my dashboard and he rereads it every morning on the way to school. This is a practice of internalization that will eventually become an identification of purpose.

Turn the page.

Future
ˈfyo͞oCHər/
noun
the time or a period of time following the moment of
speaking or writing; time regarded as still to come.

FUTURE. Due to the existence of time and the law of physics, the future is inevitable. Meaning we will come face to face with the future at some present point in time.

Coupled with that meet up is our collective past of decisions, choices, and habits. When you look your future square in the eye what will be before you? Will it be riddled with regret or bountiful? Take a moment and acknowledge what could potentially be your future based on your current mindset.

There was a point in my life where I regarded the future as something far in the distance that I was smart enough to make up for just in the nick of time. Boy was I wrong. With every tick of the clock we are witnessing the evolution of the past, present, and future. Therefore, every single moment matters. Whether we like it or not. When we make a commitment to make sound, intentional decisions our future selves thank us and so will our children and our children's children.

Thinking versus doing. A word to the wise, it is not enough to just sit and daydream about your future. You have to put those desires into action with a plan. We do this by determining the steps to take in order to put the plan in motion.

Remember time is constantly in motion; either you will run into it head on as a productive force to be reckoned with or it will meet you in a state of stagnation. There is a life management concept, the four D's, that pinpoints exactly what I am referring to. Do it, delegate it, delay it, or drop it. The power is in your hands.

Growth application:

There are 24 hours in one day and there are 8,760 hours in one year. If you have a full time job that equates to 40 hours per week worked with a standard 2 week vacation that means you spend approximately 2,000 hours at work in one year. Can you account for the other 6,760 remaining hours that you have been given? Take some time to think about your future. Write out what that looks like. Now put some movement behind that and do something with those hours that will catapult you and your family into another dimension.

Turn the page.

Generation

ˌjenəˈrāSH(ə)n/

noun

all of the people born and living at about the same time, regarded collectively.

GENERATION. No doubt each generation living or dead is born into a specific set of circumstances that become representative of such. The most commonly discussed generations presently are the baby boomers and the millennials. There seems to be this ever present rift between identifying any commonalities and more so the magnitude of differences. This can be widely attributed to the boom in technology, globalization, and exponential economic growth – and decline if you were anywhere around during the 2008 debacle.

I shed light on this because generational differences become very prominent in financial management. Goals and desires make themselves known in the approach and attitude towards wealth building within the experience of each economic event. Every generation has its pain point and depending on when you were born you may be more susceptible to financial shortfalls if you are unaware of the hand you have been dealt.

Thinking back to the financial habits of my grandparents, born during the era of the Great Depression, their lifestyles were built on a foundation of solid work ethic and simplicity. For the Traditional or Silent Generation output always equaled input. They went to work, purchased a home, saved for leisure activities, sent their children to college and retired with a pension. Not so simple for Baby Boomers and Gen Xers. These two generations both experienced the first taste of economic disparity across class systems. The ease of affording, attaining and maintaining the American dream has not always been held with a tight grip. These were also the generations where it became common to have a dual income household and women began to insert themselves in arenas that were traditionally occupied by their male counterparts. And then we have the

Millennials. The generation that is widely known for their entrepreneurial, fast paced, output generated at light speed, moving and shaking temperament. The collision of all four of these generations is ever present during the twenty first century as many American households are representative of multi-generational living. This fact alone can be great for coffee table conversations and passing on fundamental financial principles if there is an awareness of each of the generational value systems.

The following box identifies four generations and their characteristics. Use this as a guideline when strategizing your financial plan across generations. Where do you fit in?

Millennials	Generation X
Born 1981 to 2004 Ages: 12-35 Tech savvy Optimistic	Born 1965 to 1980 Ages: 36-51 Cynical Independent
Primary financial goals: managing student loan debt and saving	Primary financial goals: build or rebuild wealth
Economic event pain points: student debt, tough job market	Economic event pain points: housing crisis, heavy debt
Baby Boomers	**Traditionalists**
Born 1946 to 1964 Ages: 52-70 Ambitious Competitive	Born 1926 to 1945 Ages: 70+ Hard Working Thrifty
Primary financial goals: prepare for retirement	Primary financial goals: Preservation of retirement savings
Economic event pain points: wealth loss during housing crisis, inadequate retirement savings	Economic event pain points: overspending in retirement, rising healthcare costs

Adapted from: https://www.wealthmanagement.com Different Generations: Different Goals

Growth application:

How often have you heard the phrase: "Kids these days?" Have you slipped into the generation where you are now saying it? I know I have. That phrase does us no good if we are not actively bridging the divide between ourselves and our children so that the transfer of wealth can take place successfully. Looking at the previous chart what can you identify about your own upbringing compared to each generation's characteristics? How have they helped or hindered your financial growth? Let's work to complete the phrase "Kids these days..." with a positive, sustainable affirmation by doing our part. How about, "Kids these days are so incredibly financially aware that their ability to cultivate and sustain wealth has surpassed that of any other generation."

Turn the page.

Legacy

ˈleɡəsē/

noun

a thing handed down by a predecessor.

LEGACY. "The only question with wealth is what you do with it. It can be used for evil purposes or it can be an instrumentality for constructive social living." - John D Rockefeller Jr

When we make reference to or think of the wealthiest people in the world, I mean the wealthiest of the wealthy, you know those household names – those people that we all call on when we are describing our aspirations or goals of living our best lives, who comes to mind? Perhaps the Rockefeller family, the Walton family, the Du Pont family, the Hearst family, the Goldman family, the Gallo family, the S.C. Johnson family, the King Family, the Kennedy family, the Obama Family, the Winfrey family, the Carter Family or the Gates family, and I would say the list goes on and on – but it doesn't.

More important than elite buying power, is the story your family name upholds. The names on the list tell the narrative of an individual that had the courage to do something so extraordinarily different for their time, and leveraged opportunities that were granted to them over generations.

However, when it comes to establishing a legacy, one comes to a fork in the road. The choice must be made between an individual legacy and a familial legacy. I would argue (and agree with Aristotle) that the whole is greater than the sum of its parts. And in order to establish a familial legacy, we must consider what we want to be spoken of our name by the generation of our grandchildren's children.

Have you ever taken the time to envision what will be representative three or four notches up on your family tree? I don't believe I will come across anyone that, even in a split moment, when stretching their imagination a century down the road that does not desire to see a life of abundant wealth and prosperity. Personally, when I have done this I catch myself smiling; full of immense hope and desire. But, hope and desire is just the gateway to achieving this. I remember doing projects in elementary school where we were instructed to create a family crest. As a sense of pride, the crest was representative of what your family stood for, fought for and achieved; and was passed down from generation to generation.

Perhaps you desire for your family legacy to be built from the foundation of social justice, or advocating for educational equality, or philanthropic endeavors, or even entertainment. Whatever it may be, make the choice today in order to begin to cultivate tomorrow's story.

Growth application:

Typically the coat of arms was passed down to the males in the familial lineage. We no longer live in the Medieval Age and the legacy that you create for your family is carried by all that will come after you. What characteristics would you like to be representative of your family coat of arms? If your legacy was an image divided into four parts what would it consist of?

If you do not like the present picture it's time to leverage your power and change it. The thought behind this is imperative because all families have a set of values and beliefs. These beliefs and values are then passed down from generation to generation and become a part of each generation's worldview. With a clear purpose of building your legacy, take an inventory of which family values you will choose to discard, modify or keep.

Turn the page.

PART V

~

RE-EXAMINING

Accumulation

əˌkyo͞om(y)əˈlāSH(ə)n/

noun

the acquisition or gradual gathering of something.

ACCUMULATION. When is the last time you paused to watch a squirrel at a park? Living in California you cannot go one day without seeing those little furry creatures running up a tree or darting across the street. I would say that the most interesting thing to observe a squirrel in the process of is exercising their accumulation strategy. They spend a huge chunk of their time gathering nuts from trees and running off to stash them away. Where there stash is located, we'd probably never find with the naked human eye. However, they know exactly where they drop these nuts and each location where they are stored. Yes, squirrels have different storage locations! Why do they do this you might be asking? It's simple, it's a protection mechanism for what they have accumulated – protection from natural disaster and from other animals. During seasons of abundance squirrels accumulate what they need to hold them over in barren months. This is a cycle that they repeat year after year. Their survival depends on it.

Similarly, we spend most of our adult lives afforded the opportunity to accumulate enough to serve as provision during the barren times. This is less about earning billions of dollars and more about your mentality towards preparation. It's all relative. The squirrel has a perpetual daily goal. This goal is driven by one thing; surrendering to the need to prepare. Seasons are inevitable and while depending on the year some seasons may yield an overabundance of fruit, but we also know that winter is coming. Not all winters are wrought with devastation but there is no way to predict the magnitude of suffering due to the lack of preparation. What are your methods of accumulation? Do your daily efforts contribute to your long term goals in an impactful way or is it more like throwing a dart with a blind fold on?

The term accumulation originates from a Latin word meaning to heap up. Whatever your personal goals are for accumulation there is a way that you can "heap up" successfully.

Things to consider:

Is your storage container suitable for what you are gathering? Keep in mind the different locations the squirrel chooses to stash his goods.

Have you been focused daily on your long term goal? Not a day goes by that the squirrel does not gather something for his future.

Where do you spend your time? What good would it do for the squirrel to forage for nuts in a place that had little to no trees? Where are the nuts that will add to your heap?

Growth application:

Did you know that there is such a thing as waste accumulation? Concerning the environment, the accumulation of waste is destructive to the atmosphere and even trickles down into having a negative impact on the economy. While the type of accumulation I referenced previously refers to positive preparation we should spend some time evaluating those things, habits, and resources that we have accumulated over time that have a negative correlation to our long term goals. When is the last time you got rid of some things that no longer contribute to your desired results?

Turn the page.

Preservation

ˌprezərˈvāSH(ə)n/

noun

the action of preserving something.

pre·serve

prəˈzərv/

verb

maintain (something) in its original or existing state.

PRESERVATION. One of the most prevalent goals of the clients that I have served over the years is preservation of the wealth that they have accumulated - and of course finding ways to grow beyond the principal. Most of the time when people think of investing they will admit that they want the opportunity of a return on their investment but without the risk of losing the initial capital that they choose to put up. There are certain options that completely protect your original investment while there are others that risk your ability to preserve anything. Where you fall on that spectrum is an individual realization. When it comes to preservation there is an intrinsic value placed on what you have acquired. This determination in value compared to a desired reward is what drives your ability to take on risk.

The main ally to preservation is the other "p" word. Protection.

Think about things we like to protect. If you own a home or a car you probably have an alarm system. If you own a cell phone more than likely you've purchased insurance. You might have a tag or a chip on your pet in case they are lost or stolen. There are plenty of things in our lives that we are completely protective over due to our desire to preserve what we have acquired. And in the case of an unfortunate circumstance like a home invasion or catastrophic disaster without insurance you are at a complete loss.

Have you ever experienced the devastation of losing something you weren't proactive about preserving through protection? We may gripe and complain about the extra cost, the extra amount of paperwork, or even the extra time that it takes to ensure the preservation of our assets but it is undeniably worth it. What is the first thing that comes to mind if you see a car on the road that has clearly been involved in an auto accident but still being driven? Perhaps they did not have auto insurance. And just like that the need for protection is realized. Accidents happen. Unfortunate circumstances occur. What we don't know is the how, when, and what of these ordeals. If there were a crystal ball that forewarned us then so many would not have suffered from the perils of the 2008 economic crisis.

In order to preserve what you have worked so hard for you must devise a plan of protection for what is valuable to you.

Start a list of valuables you want to preserve and your method of protection. **A word to the wise**: People count too.

Preserve	Protection method
1. *My home*	*Homeowners insurance*
2. *Standard of living*	*Retirement accounts*
3.	

Growth application:

When you do not feel protected as a human being then symptoms of vulnerability creep in. You may become fearful or even stagnant. Downright afraid to move. Consider your financial decisions and the level of protection this offers you and your family. Do these decisions align with what you are attempting to preserve?

Often time complacency is the main culprit to our lack of protective measures. Residing in comfortability is where we begin to take for granted the things we were once vigilant about.

Turn the page.

Stewardship
ˈst(y)o͞oərdˌSHip/
noun
the job of supervising or taking care of something, such as
an organization or property, the arrangements for a group or the
resources of a community. *especially*: the careful and
responsible management of something entrusted to one's care

STEWARDSHIP. There are many representations of the term stewardship. The theological belief that as a human beings we are positioned as caretakers of the world seems to spill over into all of the remaining personifications.

Stewardship requires a level of responsibility that holds what is being cared for in highest of regard. If you are a parent, then you are stewards over your children and responsible for the management and care of their wellbeing. If you serve on the Board of Directors of a company or as the trustee of an organization you have been entrusted with the fiduciary responsibility of maintaining the wellbeing of the organization. If you are the head of your household you have inherited the task of financial stewardship over your family's resources. The concept of stewardship can be swept across our lives with a broad brush, however, the success of it lies within the value we place on what we have been granted to manage.

Good stewardship encompasses ethics of responsibility, accountability and reward. This is especially simple to adhere to if you hold the view that what you are managing extends well beyond a personal benefit. Your children will grow up to be productive citizens, the organization you lead will continue to do good work for the community they serve, your family legacy will be one of financial abundance when the level of responsibility and accountability are maintained.

Understanding the importance of stewardship can easily start at a young age and be coupled with teaching the art of good decision making. Think about some of the most important decisions you have had to make in your life. I could be wrong, but I would argue that many of these decisions boil down to weighing the value that you place on one thing over the other. Make a short list of the last five important decisions you have had to make and what resource was used to achieve them.

Growth application:

As a parent one of the hardest yet rewarding ways to teach your children about stewardship, in my opinion, is allowing them to have a pet. Each of my children at some point have literally pleaded for a pet of some kind. And after a while, when the thrill is gone, the vigilance in maintenance declines and somehow shifts to me as the caretaker. This has been one of my easiest teaching opportunities. I continuously remind them that the pet is what they have been entrusted to manage because of their expressed desires and I will be there merely to serve as a support system. How often, even in the financial legacy you desire to impart on your families have you dropped the ball when the newness of what you are building wears off? The vitality of your legacy depends on how well you do your job of taking care of it.

Turn the page.

Choices
CHois/
noun
an act of selecting or making a decision when faced with
two or more possibilities.

CHOICES. I stand firm on the fact that you have the power to choose whatever it is that you want to do. But, what you cannot dictate are the consequences of those choices. Each day that we open our eyes your slate of decision making commences. The process to making these decisions is what will dictate each successive option.

Often times the outcomes to our choices do not reflect immediately, and instead make a pop up appearance months or years later. In the finance industry, professionals pride themselves on making "informed" decisions and likewise, passing down that information to the investor in order for them to ultimately make a choice suitable for implementation. These decisions are intentionally executed for the best possible outcome given the supplied information.

Making good decisions is not a skill that is acquired from birth, and instead is a learned behavior honed over a lifetime of experiences. While some choices presented before us are easy, many will not be. Designing a thoughtful process for those life changing decisions can serve as a buffer to costly outcomes.

Think about the following the next time you are asked to choose:

What and why am I choosing?
What are the alternatives?
How does this choice affect me now? In the future?
What have I decided?
Was this a good decision?

Growth application:

I can remember wavering in a lot of my choices as a child and a young adult. None of these were life threatening but rested in the lack of surety in the outcome. Now that I have done the work of what I have also shared with you, I realize that the lack of confidence was in my process. I had no process. Therefore, there was nothing solid to put my mind at ease once a decision was made. The lack of a substantial process induces worry and stress, and can ultimately stunt your outcome. If this has been you, you owe it to yourself to design a process that you are comfortable with and commit to it.

Turn the page.

Freedom

ˈfrēdəm/

noun

the power or right to act, speak, or think as one wants
without hindrance or restraint.
the state of not being imprisoned or enslaved.
the power of self-determination attributed to the will; the
quality of being independent of fate or necessity.

FREEDOM. What is the financial backdrop that your life was founded upon or that you inherited that recognizably has shaped your future? What were you taught about the meaning and purpose of money? What were you taught about wealth? What is it that you would like to declare differently for your financial future? At this point the answers are probably a lot clearer to you.

As stated in the Declaration of Independence, it is within your right "that whenever any form of government becomes destructive of these ends, it is the Right of the People to alter or to abolish it, and to institute new Government, laying its foundation on such principles and organizing its powers in such form, as to them shall seem most likely to affect their safety and happiness..."

...and as stated in the **Declaration of *your* Financial Independence,** it is within *your right* that whenever any form of financial practice becomes destructive of these ends, it is the right of the people to alter or to abolish it, and to institute new Financial values, laying its foundation on such principles and organizing its powers in such form, as to them shall seem most likely to affect their financial safety and happiness.

The financial freedom of your future generations depends on what YOU declare today. The right to act, speak and think about this is inherent in *your* freedom. Broadly speaking, taking the liberty to do as one pleases is the ultimate measure of freedom and often times what holds us in bondage are not the realities of what others have encroached upon us but the narratives we impose upon ourselves. There are common fears that tend to restrict our lives: the fear of uncertainty, loneliness, change, fear of the loss of freedom – or modernly referred to as FOMO (fear of missing out), the fear of being judged or that we are inadequate; and the list could go on and on. Fear has the ability to hold you back in almost every area of your life – if *you* allow it.

It is most important to recognize that fear is a basic human emotion; it is hard wired into all of our systems. We need this emotion to signal us in times of eminent danger. Think of it as the precursor to an action packed moment centered on our ability to survive. At its best, fear is necessary. But what about when it is unwarranted?

Often times when we are fueled by unwarranted fear our judgment becomes skewed and ultimately prevents our ability to think clearly through circumstances. These fears stem from negative experiences and are typically coupled with a feeling of loss of control. One of the most recent financial examples that highlights this is the Great Recession of 2008. While hesitation to re-engage in the financial markets by those who were impacted is understood, inaction ultimately leads to stifled growth.

A breakthrough requires that you release your interpretations of past experiences and teachings. Instead, make a choice to begin to cultivate your legacy without restraint; moving from fear to freedom.

Turn the page.

"I am not a product of my circumstances.
I am a product of my decisions."
– Stephen Covey

EPILOGUE

And just like that you have done it. You have explored thirty different words on the journey to renewing your mind and are well on your way to building a lasting legacy. Just to be clear, your wealth path did not start when you purchased this book. You were placed at your starting point the day you were born. What you have done with this book is committed yourself to renewal. To renew means to re-establish something. We reestablished our processes and behavioral patterns revolving around legacy building. When we renew we also make fresh or strong again. The key point to hone in on is the "again" part. This means that it was present before and now it has been revived. Congratulations on your strength, perseverance, and dedication to do so.

My hope is that you have grown thirty words wiser and your family will benefit exponentially from your knowledge. Because of this, I want to challenge you to revisit these words often. Your legacy is worth the commitment.

Onward.

About the author

Andrea Collins is a Portfolio Analyst at an investment management firm in Beverly Hills, specializing in intelligently personalized portfolio management for high-net-worth individuals, families, and foundations. Since 2005, she has dedicated her career to working closely with each client's advisor to developing portfolios based on the client's investment objective, time horizon, income needs, and tolerance for market volatility.

Noting that wealth management is not only for affluent individuals she has dedicated more than a decade to designing a straightforward process to achieving optimal results.

Active in the community she frequently teaches financial literacy workshops for schools and organizations in an effort to create a multi-generational understanding of financial stewardship, wealth management, and legacy building.

www.ingramcontent.com/pod-product-compliance
Lightning Source LLC
Chambersburg PA
CBHW020039040426
42331CB00030B/79